RETIREMENT BOOK FOR WOMEN OVER 50

Golden Years: A Woman's Guide to Life After 50, Investing wisely, Health and wellness, Evolving and Planning Your Ideal Retirement

Brandon Oliver

Brandon Oliver

Copy Right ©2024 Brandon Oliver

All Rights Reserved

TABLE OF CONTENTS

TABLE OF CONTENTS	**2**
INTRODUCTON	**5**
CHAPTER 1	**7**
HOW RETIREMENT FUNCTIONS	**7**
Retirement Age	8
Why retirement planning is essential for women over 50	9
Challenges Faced by Women in Retirement	15
CHAPTER 2	**19**
FINANCIAL RETIREMENT PLANNING FOR INDIVIDUALS 45–54 YEARS OLD	**20**
CHAPTER 3	**33**
HOW TO MANAGE DEBT IN RETIREMENT	**33**
Types of Debt	34
Managing Debt Payments in Retirement	36
CHAPTER 4	**41**
INVESTMENT STRATEGIES FOR WOMEN OVER 50	**41**
Defining your legacy: a woman's perspective	48
CHAPTER 5	**51**

IMPORTANCE OF WELLNESS IN RETIREMENT 51

CHAPTER 6 63

TRANSITION TO RETIREMENT 63
How to avoid loneliness and isolation during retirement 69

CHAPTER 7 73

WORKING AFTER RETIREMENT 73
Regarding medical retirement 75
10 Best Jobs for Retirees 76

CHAPTER 8 85

REASONS FOR RETIREMENT COMMUNITIES 85

CHAPTER 9 91

BENEFITS OF RETIREMENT TRAVEL 91

CONCLUSION 95

INTRODUCTON

A comprehensive guide designed to equip you with the knowledge and strategies necessary to confidently approach your retirement years. As a woman over 50, you stand at a pivotal moment in your life one where thoughtful planning can significantly impact your financial security and overall well-being in the years ahead.

In this book, we focus into the unique considerations that women face when preparing for retirement. From the gender pay gap to caregiving responsibilities, this book talk about the various factors that can influence your financial future and offer practical advice tailored to your specific needs.

Throughout these pages, you'll discover actionable steps to assess your current financial situation, set achievable retirement goals, and develop a personalized plan to work towards them. Whether you're just beginning to think about retirement or are already on the cusp of this new chapter, this book will serve as a valuable resource to help you go through the complexities of retirement planning with confidence and clarity.

CHAPTER 1

HOW RETIREMENT FUNCTIONS

Retirement, a relatively modern notion, emerged alongside longer life expectancies. Just over a hundred years ago, retirement wasn't even a concept. It gradually evolved due to longer lifespans, the rise of pension plans in specific sectors, and the inception of government-backed benefits in 1935 with Social Security.

Deciding when to retire is significantly an individual choice. Equally important is figuring out how much to spend during retirement. Additionally, you'll need to determine when to begin receiving Social Security benefits. Delaying Social Security payments can lead to a higher monthly payout down the road.

If you have a pension, you'll face crucial decisions, such as opting for a lump sum or an annuity, and selecting the terms, like a lifetime benefit for yourself or ongoing support for your spouse in case of your premature demise.

Retirement Age

Unlike some countries, the United States doesn't enforce a mandatory retirement age. However, the Social Security Administration sets rules regarding the timing of retirement benefits, which can influence your payout and should be factored into your plans. While 65 are generally considered the standard retirement age, Social Security calculates your full retirement age based on your birthdate, which varies for each individual. Retiring before 60 is typically seen as early retirement, with the IRS often penalizing retirement plan withdrawals before age 59½. Yet, exceptions exist for scenarios like military service, medical needs, disability, and more.

Why retirement planning is essential for women over 50

Entering your 50s feels like hitting a stride. You're likely at the peak of your career, surrounded by a solid support system, and brimming with confidence, guided by five decades of life lessons.

This phase marks a crucial juncture for personal growth, wealth building, and gearing up for what lies ahead: retirement.

Imagine retirement planning in your 50s as cruising down an open road, the wind in your hair, and the sun on your face pure freedom to carve out your own path toward the future.

Here's a solid approach to bolster your retirement blueprint in your 50s, start envisioning your ideal retirement lifestyle. Consider these three tips:

Set Your Goals

While many people in their 50s focus on the financial aspects of retirement, emotional readiness often takes a back seat. According to Greenwald Diversified Services, 74% of individuals aged 50-59 diligently plan financially for retirement, yet only 35% give equal attention to emotional preparation. Setting goals that set your retirement aspirations is paramount.

As retirement looms, start sketching out tangible goals for your golden years. What excites you most about retirement? Do you envision endless hours tending to your garden or globetrotting? Your aspirations can shape your transition and solidify objectives, whether it's being closer to family or

Brandon Oliver

relocating to a warmer climate for year-round gardening.

Envision Your Dream Retirement

Though you've spent decades shaping your career and life, retirement might still feel a bit distant. Actively visualizing your future can rekindle motivation. Imagine yourself in your later years, reflecting deeply:

- How do you spend your days?

- What brings you purpose and joy?

Visualizing your ideal retirement can inspire habits that pave the way, like boosting savings, making prudent financial decisions, clearing debts, and prioritizing your future self.

Evaluate Your Career Path

In your 50s, you might find yourself at a career crossroads well-established but yearning for change. Reflect on these questions:

- How many more years do you envision yourself working?

Setting loose career timelines aids in financial and personal retirement planning. If an early retirement beckons, ramping up savings or revisiting spending plans might be necessary. On the flip side, extending your career by a year or two can bolster retirement accounts and Social Security benefits.

- Do you crave a career shift?

Many individuals seek fulfillment alongside financial stability in their jobs. Assess your current satisfaction level and explore potential changes. Perhaps entrepreneurship or a new field beckons. Consider the financial implications and seek guidance from a financial advisor to navigate transitions confidently.

As you map out your future, remember to strike a balance between maximizing earning potential and investing in personal growth. Retirement planning in your 50s is an exhilarating journey filled with possibilities. By crafting a lifestyle aligned with your dreams, you're laying the groundwork for a purposeful retirement ahead.

- How Much Does Retirement Cost?

There's no one-size-fits-all answer to the cost of retirement. Funding your retirement hinges on various factors, including your planned retirement age, life expectancy, and anticipated living expenses during retirement. This necessitates a personalized financial evaluation.

Planning and saving ahead are key to achieving a comfortable retirement. It's advisable to start saving early, ideally in your 20s or 30s, setting aside at least 10% of your income annually. If you commence saving later in life, say in your 40s or 50s, you'll need to stash away a larger portion of your income perhaps up to 50% per year.

Challenges Faced by Women in Retirement

Going Through Retirement Challenges for Women:

Addressing the Gender Pay Gap

The gender pay gap poses a significant hurdle for women in retirement planning. On average, women earn less than men, making it tougher to save for the future. Moreover, women often take breaks from work to raise children or care for family members, further impacting their earnings. To tackle this, it's crucial for women to advocate for higher pay. Research industry standards, be transparent with employers about your goals, and confidently negotiate for fair compensation.

For female entrepreneurs, valuing your worth and charging accordingly is key to financial stability.

Coping with Longer Life Expectancy

Women typically outlive men, necessitating more retirement savings to cover the extended lifespan. Additionally, women may face higher healthcare expenses as they age. To counter this, early retirement planning and diligent saving are vital. Start saving as early as possible and maximize employer-offered retirement plans to secure your financial future.

Overcoming Financial Confidence Issues

Many women lack confidence in financial decision-making and investing, leading to missed opportunities for growth. Education and seeking guidance from financial experts can boost confidence. Learn about investment strategies and build a diversified portfolio to feel more assured about financial choices.

Dealing with Divorce and Spousal Loss

Divorce or the death of a spouse can disrupt retirement plans, particularly if relying on a partner's savings. To safeguard against this, consider life insurance and diversify investments. Develop a financial plan that accounts for potential life changes, such as divorce or loss of a spouse.

Managing Elderly Care Costs

Women often shoulder the responsibility of caring for elderly relatives, impacting their ability to save. Planning for elderly care expenses early is crucial. Explore options like long-term care insurance and government assistance programs to alleviate financial strain.

In essence, women encounter several unique retirement challenges. However, with proactive planning, negotiation for fair pay, and seeking professional advice, women can take charge of their financial futures and build a secure retirement.

CHAPTER 2

FINANCIAL RETIREMENT PLANNING FOR INDIVIDUALS 45–54 YEARS OLD

Retirement Planning for Ages 45-54: Strategies for Success

Entering the realm between 45 and 54 years old often marks a pivotal point in one's career, where income peaks and financial responsibilities, particularly towards home and family, escalate. This juncture poses unique challenges for retirement planning. Here are six actionable tips to either maintain or bolster your retirement savings trajectory.

The Diverse Landscape

The 45-54 age bracket presents a diverse spectrum of individuals encompassing various life stages, from those with no children to new parents and empty nesters. It spans early career aspirants to seasoned professionals nearing retirement. While life stages differ across all age ranges, 45-54 stands out for its pronounced divergences.

For those within this demographic, ideally, momentum toward retirement savings goals is building. However, for those lagging, avenues exist to accelerate contributions to their retirement nest egg. These avenues include entrepreneurship, adoption of tailored retirement plans, and leveraging catch-up contributions.

Entrepreneurial Pursuits

Embarking on entrepreneurial endeavors, whether a lifelong dream or newfound aspiration, can be opportune at this juncture.

Capitalizing on personal talents or skills to generate supplementary income through a side business, while maintaining a primary job, not only boosts earnings but also facilitates the establishment and funding of a retirement plan through the business.

Depending on the chosen retirement plan, contributions could soar to significant levels. For instance, the IRS permits contributions of up to $66,000 for the 2023 tax year (rising to $69,000 for 2024), with an additional catch-up contribution of up to $7,500 annually for individuals aged 50 and above. These contributions are separate from those made under an employer's retirement plan.

Simultaneous Participation in Employer-Sponsored and Self-Employed Plans

Remarkably, the IRS sanctions contributions to both an employer's 401(k) and a self-employed retirement plan concurrently.

Contribution limits hinge on the plan type and the extent of contributions to the employer's plan.

Solo 401(k)

Tailored for businesses devoid of employees besides a spouse, the Solo 401(k) mirrors standard 401(k) contribution limits. Contributions can reach up to $22,500 in 2023 ($23,000 in 2024), with an additional catch-up contribution of $7,500 annually for individuals aged 50 and above. Employers can further contribute up to 25% of the employee's compensation, culminating in a combined maximum contribution of $66,000 in 2023 ($73,500 for those aged 50 and above) or $69,000 in 2024 ($76,500 for those aged 50 and above).

SEP IRA

The SEP IRA, tailored for self-employed individuals, allows contributions of up to 25%

of income or $66,000, whichever is lower, without provision for catch-up contributions.

To fully capitalize on these opportunities, individuals should consider consulting legal experts to determine the most suitable business structure, whether sole proprietorship, partnership, LLC, or corporation.

Harness Catch-up Contributions

For those initiating retirement savings later in life, hope is far from lost. Special provisions enable individuals aged 50 and above to bridge the gap by contributing extra funds.

Individual Retirement Accounts (IRAs)

Individuals aged 50 and above can contribute up to $6,500 for the 2023 tax year, increasing to $7,000 for 2024, or 100% of compensation, whichever is lesser.

Employer-Sponsored Plans

For plans like SIMPLE IRA, contributions can reach $15,500 for 2023 ($16,000 for 2024), with an additional catch-up contribution of $3,500 annually for those aged 50 and above. Similarly, 401(k), 403(b), and 457 plans allow contributions of up to $22,500 for 2023 ($23,000 for 2024), with a $7,500 catch-up contribution for those aged 50 and above.

Familiarize Yourself with State Laws Regarding Marriage and Divorce

Entering into or dissolving a marriage can profoundly impact your retirement savings. Marriage introduces various dynamics that can influence your retirement planning. On the positive side, combining assets and income with your spouse can enhance financial projections and potentially reduce individual savings burdens.

However, prudent financial management may dictate maintaining higher savings rates despite projected lower individual saving requirements in a married scenario, if feasible.

In the event of spousal loss without remarriage, sole responsibility for retirement funding falls upon the surviving spouse. Conversely, divorce mandates equitable distribution of retirement assets between spouses, potentially affecting individual nest eggs.

Explore Alternative Retirement Income Streams

Your 401(k) or IRA funds may not constitute your sole retirement income. Consider diversifying your income sources:

Social Security

Eligibility for Social Security retirement benefits commences at age 62, with increased benefits available upon deferral until ages 67 or 70, assuming a minimum of 10 years of work history (or eligibility through a spouse).

Employer Pension Plans

Defined benefit plans, though less prevalent, guarantee retirement income and are funded by employers. If affiliated with a company offering such plans, you may be entitled to additional retirement income.

Spousal Income or Work Record

Even without personal income, married individuals can contribute to retirement accounts using their spouse's income through spousal IRAs, facilitating continued retirement savings.

Furthermore, you may be eligible for Social Security benefits based on the work history of your current or former spouse.

Maintain Portfolio Balance

Regularly reassess your retirement nest egg's asset allocation through rebalancing. This practice allows you to evaluate whether adjustments to your asset allocation are necessary.

Approaching retirement age may prompt a shift towards less risky investments to mitigate potential losses, although individual circumstances vary. Seeking guidance from a knowledgeable financial advisor can aid in selecting a suitable asset allocation model.

Contemplate Additional Retirement Expenses

Various factors can impact retirement planning, such as decisions regarding funding children's education or supporting adult children living at home alongside prioritizing retirement savings. While investing in a child's future may seem altruistic, it could inadvertently strain your finances in retirement, potentially necessitating financial support from your children or delaying your retirement.

Additionally, consider the feasibility of purchasing long-term care insurance (LTC) to safeguard retirement savings from being depleted by expenses arising from prolonged illness, preserving funds for your envisioned retirement lifestyle.

FAQs:

How much should a 45-year-old have saved for retirement?

Retirement savings targets for a 45-year-old hinge on retirement age and desired post-retirement income. For instance, individuals earning $100,000 annually should ideally aim for savings between $330,000 and $450,000, according to Edward Jones data.

What is the recommended retirement savings for a 54-year-old?

A 54-year-old, being closer to retirement, should ideally have more substantial savings compared to a 45-year-old. For example, someone earning $100,000 annually should target savings between $585,000 and $735,000, as per Edward Jones.

What is the optimal retirement investment strategy for a 45-year-old?

Maximizing contributions to a 401(k) is often advisable due to its high contribution limit and potential employer match. Moreover, individuals aged 50 and above can make catch-up contributions, enhancing retirement savings potential.

Finally, the 45-54 age bracket marks a crucial period for bolstering retirement savings, whether by initiating entrepreneurial ventures or optimizing existing savings strategies. Whether you're just commencing your career journey or have been diligently saving for years, these retirement planning insights can prove invaluable.

CHAPTER 3

HOW TO MANAGE DEBT IN RETIREMENT

For retirees or those approaching retirement, it's prudent to reassess household debt and its impact on financial stability. While debt shouldn't necessarily derail retirement plans, evaluating overall financial health and devising a strategy to eliminate debt before retiring is advisable.

Considerations such as income, credit score, and financial circumstances can influence debt management options, including accelerated repayment, debt consolidation, or refinancing at lower interest rates. Integrating debt management into retirement planning is essential for long-term financial security.

Types of Debt

1. Credit Card Debt

Individuals in their 50s tend to carry significant credit card debt, but proactive steps can improve the situation. Increasing payments toward credit card balances is key, alongside negotiating lower interest rates or exploring balance transfer options with lower interest rates, facilitating quicker debt payoff and interest savings.

2. Mortgage Debt

While mortgage debt is often deemed favorable, retiring with a mortgage warrants a plan for repayment. Whether aiming for a debt-free home by retirement or comfortable carrying the mortgage into retirement, strategizing is vital. Options include refinancing for a shorter loan term or lower interest rate, aligning mortgage payoff with retirement goals.

For instance, if retirement is approximately a decade away and 20 years remain on the mortgage, refinancing to a 15-year mortgage with comparable monthly payments can expedite payoff.

3. Student Loans

Many parents accrue debt to support their children's education, which can linger into retirement years. While student loans are typically considered beneficial for career prospects, long-term repayment can pose challenges.

Although student loans usually cannot be discharged through bankruptcy, reviewing loan terms and discussing repayment options with children, especially if they're financially independent, can alleviate the burden.

Options may include co-signer release or arrangements for children to assume responsibility for repayment.

Managing Debt Payments in Retirement

Carrying debt into retirement doesn't necessarily mean postponing retirement plans, but it's crucial to ensure debt payments align with expected retirement income. Consider these key questions:

1. Are your debt payments manageable based on your retirement income?

2. Can you explore options like loan refinancing for lower interest rates?

3. Do you possess any high-interest bad debts, such as credit card balances?

Estimate Your Debt Levels in Retirement:

1. Calculate Expected Retirement Income: Utilize tools like the Social Security Retirement Estimator to project Social

Security benefits. Factor in any pensions, retirement account withdrawals (e.g., 401(k), IRA), annuities, or other sources of retirement income.

2. Assess Monthly Debt Obligations: Sum up monthly debt payments, encompassing mortgages, car loans, credit card bills, and other financial commitments.

3. Determine Debt-to-Income Ratio: Divide monthly debt payments by projected monthly gross retirement income. A debt-to-income ratio exceeding 43% suggests potential overextension.

Given the likelihood of reduced retirement income compared to pre-retirement earnings, aiming to live on approximately 80% of pre-retirement income is a prudent guideline. Assess whether debt payments remain manageable within this budget. If not, adjustments to retirement plans or debt reduction strategies may be necessary.

Refinancing, Consolidation, and Accelerated Debt Repayment:

For individuals grappling with substantial debt, exploring refinancing or consolidation options can provide relief:

• Cash-out refinancing of mortgages allows tapping into home equity to settle higher-interest debts like credit cards.

• Obtaining a personal loan at a lower interest rate can be used to clear high-interest credit card balances.

• Balance transfers to low introductory rate credit cards can be advantageous, but full repayment before the introductory period's end is crucial to avoid interest charges.

It's important to recognize that not all debt is inherently detrimental, and retirement doesn't mandate complete debt elimination. As long as debt payments remain manageable and a repayment strategy is in place, retirement plans need not be deferred solely due to existing debt. However, if debt concerns persist, exploring avenues for accelerated debt repayment can pave the way for a more secure retirement.

CHAPTER 4

INVESTMENT STRATEGIES FOR WOMEN OVER 50

Throughout most of your life, focusing on saving for retirement probably wasn't a top priority. But as you edge closer to the end of your career, those nerves start creeping in, and you find yourself bombarded with questions like: Have I saved enough? Was my choice to pursue aggressive investments a smart move? Do I have the right insurance coverage?

Planning for retirement isn't exactly a walk in the park, but these 10 steps offer a solid starting point:

Evaluate Your Financial Situation

Before mapping out your retirement journey, it's crucial to have a clear understanding of where you stand financially. Calculate your total net worth by subtracting your debts (like loans, mortgages, and credit card balances) from your assets (such as cash, retirement savings, and investments).

Estimate Your Future Expenses

While many believe their retirement spending will be around 70% to 80% of their pre-retirement expenses, it's essential to consider all potential costs, both planned and unexpected. Whether it's traveling the world or buying a new car, make a comprehensive list of your anticipated expenses to incorporate them into your financial plan.

Plan for Taxes

Running a tax projection can help you strategize how to manage your finances effectively, minimizing tax burdens both now and during retirement. Techniques like consolidating charitable contributions using a donor-advised fund or executing partial Roth conversions can be advantageous. Donor-advised funds allow for tax-deductible donations, while partial Roth conversions offer tax-free benefits. Business owners might also benefit from adjusting income and expenses to optimize tax outcomes, though staying updated on changing tax laws is crucial.

Decide on Partial Roth Conversions

As retirement approaches, especially within the ten years leading up to it, there's a valuable opportunity to become more tax-savvy. If a significant portion of your retirement savings resides in IRA accounts, you'll eventually encounter substantial required minimum distributions that are subject to income taxes. However, by opting for partial Roth conversions, you can strategically transfer funds from your IRA, paying taxes upfront, and enjoy tax-free income in the future. The flexibility of this approach is its key advantage it doesn't have to be an all-or-nothing decision. You can convert smaller amounts over several years, managing your tax bracket and reducing overall taxes. Nonetheless, it's essential to proceed with caution: mishandling a partial Roth conversion could lead to missed opportunities or long-term financial losses. Approach the process thoughtfully, consider using regular cash flow to cover taxes, and seek guidance from a trusted advisor to avoid costly mistakes.

Maximize Tax-Deferred Accounts and Catch-Up Contributions

Each year, the IRS establishes maximum contribution limits for retirement accounts such as IRAs and 401(k)s. For example, in 2021, the cap for 401(k) contributions is $19,500, with an additional $6,500 permitted for individuals aged 50 and above. Meanwhile, traditional and Roth IRAs allow contributions of up to $6,000 for those under 50, and $7,000 for those 50 and older. Utilizing these higher limits is crucial, especially if your employer provides matching contributions. If you find yourself in a situation where you no longer earn income but your spouse does, consider a spousal IRA to continue contributing. These increased limits offer an opportunity to inject more funds into your retirement savings, resulting in greater rewards in the future.

Address Your Debt

Recent data indicates that older households carry more debt than ever before. To prevent debt from overshadowing your retirement years, begin paying it off now. Start by tackling high-interest debts like credit card balances or personal loans, employing methods such as the debt avalanche technique. This approach becomes particularly critical as retirement nears, aiming to eliminate as much debt as possible before you stop working. However, refrain from tapping into your retirement accounts to settle debts the taxes incurred might outweigh any interest savings. If you still have a mortgage, consider refinancing to lower interest costs over time, but carefully evaluate the closing costs to ensure it's financial advantageous in the long term.

Refine Your Retirement Budget

Rather than simply budgeting, consider crafting a retirement spending plan. This plan allows for allocating funds for indulgences like travel or hobbies. Envision your ideal retirement lifestyle and estimate the associated expenses. By aligning your spending plan with your retirement aspirations, you'll be better equipped to manage your finances during your golden years. Anticipate fluctuations in your income, potential passive income sources, and any external support from family members. Documenting your responses to these questions can significantly enhance your retirement income planning.

Choose Best Healthcare Choices

Healthcare costs are an inevitable aspect of retirement. On average, a 65-year-old couple can anticipate spending around $11,000 on healthcare in their first year of retirement. Given this, selecting a healthcare plan with comprehensive coverage is crucial. While Medicare becomes available at 65, it may not cover all expenses, prompting many retirees to opt for supplemental Medigap insurance. These policies, provided by private insurers, can assist in covering deductibles, copayments, and other out-of-pocket costs not covered by Medicare. Choosing the right healthcare plan entails evaluating various options based on your needs and considering factors like location. Additionally, utilizing a health savings account (HSA) can offer valuable tax advantages, facilitating the coverage of healthcare expenses in retirement.

Defining your legacy: a woman's perspective

Establishing an estate strategy is crucial for women to ensure that their assets are handled according to their wishes. Below are some key points to consider:

Misconceptions about estate planning: Many people believe that having a Will is sufficient, but it only take effect upon death and doesn't protect against incapacity. Additionally, estate planning is not just for the wealthy; it's about ensuring your wishes are carried out and reducing the burden on loved ones.

Benefits of an estate strategy: An estate plan gives you control over how your assets are handled, preserves their value by minimizing taxes and expenses, and makes things easier for your family by clearly outlining your wishes.

Common tools in estate planning: It's essential to educate yourself about various estate planning tools and discuss them with an estate-planning lawyer. Some common tools include:

Health care directive or living will: Allows you to specify your health care wishes if you become unable to make decisions.

Health care power of attorney: Enables you to appoint someone to make medical decisions on your behalf.

Trust: Can be used to support charities, dictate asset distribution to heirs, and provide guidelines for asset management.

By taking the time to understand estate planning options and creating a comprehensive estate strategy, women can ensure their legacy is protected and their wishes are honored.

CHAPTER 5
IMPORTANCE OF WELLNESS IN RETIREMENT

Ensuring comprehensive retirement planning is crucial for achieving complete financial freedom in your golden years. Nevertheless, without good physical health to relish it, the envisioned quality of life remains unattainable. The enjoyment of retirement isn't solely determined by wealth; it's the amalgamation of health and financial stability that maximizes independence and freedom. Here are some strategies to uphold or enhance your overall well-being as you relish your financial independence.

What Constitutes Wellness?

Wellness, according to the Global Wellness Day organization, denotes a state characterized by health, happiness, and prosperity, extending beyond mere physical well-being to encompass mental health, social connections, and overall life satisfaction. While crafting a retirement strategy addresses financial wellness, it's incumbent upon individuals to nurture other facets of well-being.

Addressing Wellness during Retirement

We'll explore three key dimensions of wellness: mental health, social connections, and physical well-being, elucidating their significance in retirement and offering suggestions for maintenance and enhancement.

Mental Well-being

Retirement often beckons the temptation to switch off mentally after years of problem-solving in the workforce. While relaxation is appealing, sustaining mental acuity is vital to stave off cognitive decline and derive lasting enjoyment from retirement. Incorporating mental exercises into daily routines can help maintain sharpness and prolong cognitive vitality.

One effective strategy is pursuing employment during retirement, even on a part-time basis. Research from 2009 revealed that retirees engaged in work exhibited levels of well-being akin to younger non-retirees, with some evidence suggesting work can mitigate cognitive decline. A study involving nearly half a million retirees found that each additional year of work correlated with a 3.2% reduction in dementia risk.

Other activities conducive to mental agility in retirement include:

- Learning a musical instrument
- Acquiring a new language

- Engaging in journaling

- Reading

- Solving puzzles and playing games

Social Well-being

Isolation and loneliness pose significant challenges, particularly for older adults. Retirement often entails leaving behind daily interactions with coworkers, and relocating to retirement communities may result in distancing from neighbors, friends, and family. Prolonged isolation can engender feelings of detachment, both physically and psychologically, affecting overall well-being. Over 8 million adults aged 50 and above grapple with isolation, which can have health repercussions comparable to smoking 15 cigarettes daily.

Fortunately, there are numerous avenues to discover social fulfillment in retirement, though they necessitate initiative and effort on your part. Consider these options:

- Engaging in community volunteering
- Seeking a roommate for companionship
- Enrolling in or teaching classes
- Pursuing outdoor hobbies or passions

Now, let's get into the realm of physical wellness.

Physical Wellness: Use It or Lose It

The adage use it or lose it is particularly pertinent when it comes to preserving physical wellness during retirement. Aging entails inherent physical changes such as metabolic slowdown, weakened immune systems, and muscle mass loss. Yet, succumbing to a perpetual state of relaxation in retirement may exacerbate these challenges. Prioritizing physical self-care is crucial, as it can mitigate both physical and cognitive decline, thereby enhancing overall well-being. Below are some strategies to maintain physical wellness in retirement:

- Participating in exercise classes

- Tending to gardening and yard maintenance

- Adopting a canine companion for regular walks

- Enjoying strolls in the neighborhood

- Establishing and adhering to an exercise regimen.

By placing emphasis on holistic well-being in retirement, these years can be among the most rewarding of your life. While professional assistance ensures financial stability, it's incumbent upon individuals to safeguard their overall wellness as they approach retirement.

Now, let's get into the vital role of physical fitness in upholding health and wellness.

Regular Physical Fitness: Cornerstone of a Healthy Lifestyle. Sustaining physical fitness forms the bedrock of well-being, especially during the transitional phase of retirement when individuals possess increased opportunities for self-care. Engaging in routine physical activity not only fortifies muscles and enhances cardiovascular health but also fosters mental equilibrium and longevity. From a medical standpoint, experts advocate for a minimum of 150 minutes of moderate-intensity aerobic activity or 75 minutes of vigorous-intensity aerobic activity weekly, coupled with muscle-strengthening exercises on two or more days. However, the significance of physical fitness transcends meeting these benchmarks; it embodies a comprehensive approach encompassing various dimensions of wellness.

The Synergy between Physical Fitness and Mental Well-being

The relationship between physical health and mental wellness is significant. Physical activity prompts the secretion of endorphins, neurotransmitters that induce feelings of happiness while reducing stress and anxiety. Regular physical activity can alleviate symptoms of depression and enhance overall mood. Moreover, it bolsters cognitive function and memory, fostering mental acuity and decreasing the risk of age-related cognitive decline. Activities like yoga or tai chi, blending physical movement with mindfulness and relaxation techniques, offer additional mental health benefits by promoting serenity and inner tranquility.

Emphasizing Strength Training and Flexibility

While cardiovascular exercise is pivotal for heart health, strength training and flexibility exercises are equally indispensable components of physical fitness. Strength training aids in building and preserving muscle mass, crucial for a healthy metabolism and warding off age-related muscle decline. Additionally, it enhances balance and diminishes the risk of falls, a prevalent concern for older adults. Flexibility exercises, such as stretching or yoga, enhance joint mobility and muscle suppleness, mitigating injury risks and bolstering overall physical performance. A holistic fitness regimen combining cardiovascular exercise, strength training, and flexibility exercises is pivotal for comprehensive health and wellness.

Exploring Diverse Fitness Options

Finding Personalized Solutions, physical fitness isn't a one-size-fits-all endeavor. Individuals possess diverse preferences, abilities, and constraints, necessitating exploration of varied fitness options to discover what resonates best with their circumstances. Some may favor low-impact activities like swimming or cycling, while others may gravitate towards group fitness classes or outdoor pursuits such as hiking or gardening. Prioritizing enjoyable and sustainable activities is paramount for long-term adherence. For instance, individuals concerned about joint discomfort may opt for low-impact exercises like water aerobics or elliptical training. Listening to the body and adjusting the fitness routine accordingly is crucial for injury prevention and overall well-being.

Establishing Attainable Goals and Monitoring Progress

Setting realistic fitness objectives is pivotal for sustaining motivation and gauging progress. Whether aiming to increase daily step count, extend workout duration, or attain specific strength benchmarks, goals provide direction and a sense of achievement. Tracking progress through fitness apps, journals, or personal observations fosters accountability and celebrates milestones. Seeking support from a personal trainer or joining a fitness community offers guidance, encouragement, and camaraderie throughout the fitness journey.

Physical fitness assumes a central role in fostering health and wellness during phased retirement. Through regular exercise, encompassing both cardiovascular and strength training, and discovering enjoyable and sustainable activities, individuals can enhance their physical and mental well-being. Remember, initiating or continuing a fitness regimen yields abundant benefits worth the investment. So, lace up those sneakers, enlist a companion, and embark on a journey towards a healthier, more enriching retirement phase.

CHAPTER 6
TRANSITION TO RETIREMENT

Retirement is a milestone that elicits a spectrum of emotions, from eager anticipation to apprehension, influenced by various factors shaping individuals' attitudes, expectations, and readiness for this life phase.

Gender Dynamics

Notably, gender plays a pivotal role in shaping retirement perceptions and preparations. Research underscores significant disparities between men and women in their approach to retirement. Generally, men exhibit a more positive outlook and greater engagement in retirement planning compared to women. Women often grapple with uncertainties in retirement readiness, stemming from historical and individual differences in labor market participation. As primary caregivers, women bear additional responsibilities, leading to precarious financial situations and heightened reliance on their and their partners' health for retirement planning. Moreover, women tend to face greater challenges in adapting to retirement than their male counterparts.

Socio-economic Factors

Perceptions of financial well-being wield considerable influence over retirement attitudes, transcending actual economic status. Individuals with a more favorable financial outlook are inclined to proactively plan for retirement. Conversely, those from disadvantaged socio-economic backgrounds tend to report more negative retirement experiences, underscoring the intertwined nature of financial security and retirement satisfaction.

Ethno-cultural Dynamics

While limited research exists on ethnic and cultural variances in retirement, preliminary findings suggest nuanced differences. Some studies indicate that individuals from ethno cultural minorities harbor more optimistic retirement expectations, albeit with less proactive planning and heightened economic vulnerability post-retirement.

Family Dynamics

Family dynamics, particularly marital status, exert a profound impact on retirement preparedness and well-being. Marriage correlates positively with retirement planning, with collaborative efforts between spouses facilitating the transition. However, existing research predominantly focuses on heterosexual couples, overlooking insights into same-sex partnerships.

Health Status

Health plays a pivotal role in retirement decisions and planning. Individuals with health issues often opt for early retirement, potentially impacting their retirement preparedness negatively. However, those with disabilities tend to engage in more meticulous retirement planning. Early retirement due to health issues may impede adjustment to retirement.

Attitudes towards Aging

Perceptions of aging profoundly influence retirement choices. Workplace ageism can prompt older workers, particularly men, to retire prematurely. Conversely, positive attitudes towards aging correlate with better retirement planning and a propensity for early retirement.

Work and Profession

The nature of one's profession and workplace dynamics significantly shape retirement timing and experiences. Workers with limited autonomy are prone to early retirement. Moreover, when work constitutes a significant aspect of identity, retirement may provoke conflict and anxiety.

Preparation and Sense of Control

Preparation for retirement is essential for fostering a sense of control and mitigating negative effects and stress. However, studies indicate widespread unpreparedness for retirement, exacerbating challenges, particularly for individuals experiencing cognitive decline associated with aging. Cognitive decline can profoundly impact retirement planning and the perception of control over one's future.

How to avoid loneliness and isolation during retirement

Retirement presents unique challenges, from managing abundant free time to adjusting to reduced social interactions. However, it also offers ample opportunities for personal growth and fulfillment. Here are some tips to adapt to retirement and make the most of this transformative phase:

Volunteer: Find a cause close to your heart and get involved with a local nonprofit organization. Whether it's organizing a food drive, mentoring youth, or building community infrastructure, volunteering connects you with like-minded individuals and gives you a sense of purpose.

Enroll in a Class: Never stop learning! Take advantage of lifelong learning opportunities by enrolling in classes at a community college or adult education center. Whether you're interested in art, history, or technology, continuing education keeps your mind sharp and introduces you to new perspectives.

Join a Club: Connect with others who share your interests by joining a club or group. Whether it's a book club, hiking group, or hobby enthusiasts, participating in group activities fosters social connections and keeps you engaged with your passions.

Try a New Hobby: Explore new interests and hobbies that you've always wanted to pursue. Whether it's learning to play a musical instrument, experimenting with photography, or delving into arts and crafts, retirement is the perfect time to unleash your creativity and explore your passions.

Get Active: Prioritize physical activity to maintain your health and well-being in retirement. Whether it's taking daily walks, joining a fitness class, or exploring outdoor activities like hiking or biking, staying active boosts your mood, reduces feelings of loneliness, and enhances overall quality of life.

Embrace this new chapter of your life with enthusiasm and curiosity, and remember that retirement is an opportunity to discover new interests, make meaningful connections, and prioritize your well-being.

CHAPTER 7
WORKING AFTER RETIREMENT

Retirement symbolizes freedom, a culmination of years of hard work and financial planning. With a solid pension pot and the prospect of a State Pension, you have the autonomy to live life on your terms. While some may contemplate early retirement, many are opting to continue working in some capacity, either due to personal preference or financial considerations. Planning for this transition often begins in one's 50s, as retirement looms closer, with some even reentering the workforce to cope with escalating living expenses.

Working in retirement has its pros and cons. On one hand, it provides a continued income stream and the opportunity to bolster retirement savings, including employer contributions. Conversely, it may entail stress and a reluctance to commit to demanding work hours, potentially overshadowing the allure of newfound freedom.

Returning to work after retirement isn't uncommon and can be a chance to embark on a new career path or pursue previously unexplored interests. Retraining, like Mick's transition to a ski instructor post-redundancy, exemplifies the possibilities inherent in this phase of life.

Regarding the hours you can work after retirement, there are no restrictions, affording you the flexibility to tailor your workload to your preferences. Whether you choose full-time, part-time, or unpaid work, retirement grants you the liberty to shape your schedule as you see fit, embracing the freedom retirement brings.

Continuing to work after reaching retirement age offers various options to tailor your schedule according to your preferences and financial needs:

Full-Time Work

If you enjoy your current role and wish to maintain full-time employment, it's possible to continue working after retirement age. However, accessing pensions may be affected, potentially pushing you into a higher income tax band. Additionally, although you won't pay National Insurance on earnings past State Pension age, it's advisable to confirm with your pension provider about any implications.

Part-Time Work

With millions of individuals over 50 already working part-time in the UK, reducing your work hours can be a gradual transition into retirement while still earning an income. It allows for more flexibility and free time to pursue other interests or spend time with family.

Balancing Paid and Unpaid Work
Retirement offers the opportunity to strike a balance between paid employment and volunteering. Engaging in volunteer work allows you to contribute to meaningful causes, utilize your skills, and stay socially connected while also earning an income.

Regarding medical retirement
Early Medical Retirement: If health issues prevent you from continuing in your current job, early medical retirement may be an option. However, returning to work after medical retirement is feasible if your circumstances change. Keep in mind that returning to the same role may not be possible if you've already begun drawing your pension, and it could affect means-tested benefits.

As you approach retirement age, it's prudent to plan for the future and consider your ideal retirement scenario. Whether it involves a gradual transition or a clean break from work, reflecting on your preferences and expectations can help shape a fulfilling retirement journey. Keep in mind that retirement may not unfold exactly as anticipated, so remaining flexible and open to new opportunities is key.

10 Best Jobs for Retirees

Retirees often seek part-time opportunities to leverage their skills and experience without committing to full-time employment. Here are three rewarding part-time job options tailored for retirees:

1. Non-profit Consulting: Transitioning from corporate life to retirement doesn't mean giving up on stimulating work. Retirees can apply their managerial, financial, IT, or development expertise to support non-profit organizations. Whether it's fighting poverty, promoting the arts, or environmental conservation, there are various causes to align with personal interests. While compensation may not match corporate rates, the satisfaction of contributing to meaningful initiatives can be invaluable.

2. Handyman Services: For retirees who enjoy hands-on work, offering handyman services can be a lucrative option. Skilled retirees can capitalize on their tinkering abilities to assist friends, neighbors, and local businesses with various repairs and maintenance tasks. With hourly rates averaging around $50, retirees can earn extra income by tightening screws, unclogging drains, or even re-wiring circuits. Flexibility in scheduling, whether on-call or per-project basis, allows retirees to tailor their workload to their preferences.

3. Government Positions: The federal government offers promising opportunities for experienced retirees seeking part-time roles. With a significant portion of the workforce set to retire in the coming years, there is a demand for seasoned professionals to fill part-time positions. The age diversity in government roles, exemplified by the recent retirement of a 95-year-old U.S. Postal Service worker, reflects an inclusive approach to employment opportunities. Retirees can explore part-time positions across various government agencies, contributing their expertise while enjoying flexible work arrangements.

4. Tutoring: Retired educators can leverage their expertise by offering one-on-one tutoring services. With a rise in demand for test preparation tutors, particularly in subjects like math, science, and foreign languages, retirees can earn between $10 and $24 per hour. While applying to larger tutoring services like Kaplan Tutoring or Tutor.com is an option, retirees can also spread the word through their network or reach out to former colleagues and school counselors for referrals.

5. Craft Entrepreneurship: Retirees with a knack for crafting or baking can turn their hobbies into profitable ventures by selling handmade goods online. Platforms like Etsy.com provide a marketplace for artisans to showcase and sell their products. While achieving six-figure incomes may require significant dedication, retirees can still earn supplementary income by selling items they enjoy creating.

6. Retail Positions: Part-time retail jobs offer retirees the opportunity for lively interaction and supplemental income. With retailers often valuing older workers for their reliability and patience, retirees can apply for positions at shops they frequent or have a passion for. Retail jobs, especially during holidays, typically offer hourly wages around $13 along with employee discounts.

7. Temporary Office Work: Retirees with experience in finance, law, accounting, or administrative support can explore temporary office positions for extra income. Signing up with staffing agencies like Manpower or Kelly Services connects retirees with flexible work opportunities that match their skills and schedule. Additionally, retirees can consider teaming up with another retiree to apply for full-time positions on a time-sharing basis, benefiting both parties and the employer.

8. Tax Preparer: Retired accountants or individuals with strong numerical skills can consider working as tax preparers, either for established tax preparation franchises or independently. Tax preparers can earn up to

$30 per hour, especially during the busy tax season from January to April. While certification as a CPA is not mandatory, tax preparers must register with the IRS, obtain a Preparer Tax Identification Number (PTIN), and pass an IRS competency exam unless exempted.

9. Patient Advocate: Patient advocates provide non-medical home health care services to homebound individuals, assisting with daily tasks such as meal preparation, bathing, dressing, medication management, and transportation to appointments. While a nursing background is beneficial, it's not always required, as some agencies offer training programs. Part-time patient advocates can earn between $32,000 and $52,000 annually, working with agencies or directly with clients in their communities.

10. Part-Time Nurse: Retired nurses can explore part-time opportunities in home health care, particularly in continuous care for patients requiring constant medical supervision. Part-time home health nurses typically work flexible shifts ranging from four to 12 hours, covering various times of the day. Registered Nurses (RNs) and Licensed Practical Nurses (LPNs/LVNs) can earn over $60 per hour, especially in markets with high demand for assisted living facilities.

CHAPTER 8
REASONS FOR RETIREMENT COMMUNITIES

Retirement villages can be an excellent option for older women planning their retirement years. Below are some compelling reasons why:

Sense of Community and Belonging

Retirement villages offer a supportive community environment where like-minded individuals in the same stage of life can connect and build deep friendships. Regular social events, communal facilities, and group activities contribute to an active, social, and vibrant lifestyle, helping to combat isolation often experienced with aging.

Safety and Security

Safety and security are paramount concerns for older women, particularly those living alone. Retirement villages prioritize safety with comprehensive security measures and 24-hour emergency response services. Highly-trained staff members are equipped to handle emergencies, and living arrangements are tailored to older residents, reducing everyday risks.

Healthcare and Wellness Support

Many retirement villages provide on-site healthcare services, including routine check-ups, immediate medical attention, and rehabilitation services. Additionally, holistic wellness practitioners such as masseuses, therapists, yoga instructors, and mental health experts may be available to cater to residents' holistic well-being. Researching and selecting a retirement village with comprehensive healthcare amenities can address older women's often neglected healthcare needs, offering peace of mind and support for maintaining overall wellness.

Freedom and Independence

Retirement villages recognize the importance of independence for residents. They provide a balance of freedom and support, allowing individuals to manage their time and engage in activities they enjoy while ensuring assistance is available when needed. With services like maintenance, housekeeping, and gardening included, residents can focus on living life to the fullest without worrying about chores.

Personal Growth and Learning

Retirement is an opportune time for personal growth and exploration. Retirement villages offer a supportive environment for residents to pursue hobbies, interests, and learning opportunities. Whether it's through organized activities or partnerships with local educational institutions, residents have the resources to deepen their understanding and continue learning throughout their retirement years.

Financial Flexibility

Retirement villages offer a range of options to accommodate various financial situations. From rental options to buy-in communities, older women can choose a plan that aligns with their preferences and financial goals. This ensures that residents have control over their future without compromising on comfort or quality of life.

Ultimately, retirement villages provide older women with a holistic approach to retirement living, encompassing community, safety, healthcare support, personal freedom, and opportunities for growth. It's important to research and carefully consider different retirement village options to find the one that best suits individual needs and preferences, empowering older women to live vibrantly, fulfilling, and with dignity during their golden years.

CHAPTER 9

BENEFITS OF RETIREMENT TRAVEL

Traveling offers numerous benefits for overall health and well-being:

Promotes Physical Activity

Traveling often involves exploring new destinations, which naturally encourages physical activity. Whether it's walking around cities, swimming, hiking, or simply exploring landmarks, these activities contribute to increased movement and exercise. Physical activity is linked to a reduced risk of various health conditions and helps build strength to prevent falls and injuries.

Combats Social Isolation

Traveling provides opportunities to connect with others, whether it's through family vacations, friend's getaways, or meeting new acquaintances while traveling solo. Maintaining social connections is crucial for mental and emotional well-being, and intergenerational travel can be especially beneficial for both older and younger generations.

Reduces Risk of Heart Disease

Traveling often involves relaxation and unwinding, which helps reduce stress levels. Lower stress levels are associated with a decreased risk of heart issues, as elevated cortisol levels, the stress hormone, can contribute to the aging process. Studies, such as the Framingham Heart Study, have shown that regular vacations are linked to a lower chance of heart disease.

Increases Brain Health

Engaging in leisure activities that require mental effort can lower the risk of developing dementia. Traveling provides opportunities for novel experiences and problem-solving, which stimulate the brain and improve brain health. Visiting museums, historical sites, and learning new information during travel also exercises memory skills and enhances cognitive function.

Enhances Happiness

Traveling has been shown to increase happiness and decrease anxiety, with these effects often lasting even after returning home. Research indicates that experiencing new places can lead to self-reported happiness, and brain scans have shown increased activity and happiness when individuals are exposed to new experiences.

Overall, travel offers a range of physical, social, and mental benefits, making it an enjoyable and valuable activity for individuals of all ages.

CONCLUSION

Retirement Planning for Women over 50 has been written with the sole purpose of empowering you to take control of your financial future. Throughout the chapters, we've highlighted the unique challenges and opportunities that women face as they approach retirement age.

By recognizing the importance of financial independence and adopting a proactive approach to retirement planning, you've already taken the first step towards a more secure and fulfilling future. From understanding your pension options to maximizing your savings potential, you now possess the knowledge and tools to make informed decisions that align with your goals and priorities.

Note that, retirement planning is not a one size fits all endeavor. It's essential to stay flexible and adapt your strategies as your circumstances evolve. Whether you choose to continue working, pursue new hobbies, or spend more time with loved ones, your retirement should reflect your values and aspirations.

As you start his next phase of your life, know that you are not alone. Seek support from financial advisors, community resources, and trusted friends and family members to help you stay on track and conquer any challenges that may arise.

With careful planning and determination, you can embrace retirement with confidence and enjoy the freedom and security that comes with financial preparedness.

www.ingramcontent.com/pod-product-compliance
Lightning Source LLC
Chambersburg PA
CBHW050329230526
45471CB00005B/2409